AMERICA
AND ITS
CUISINE

RECIPES SELECTED AND EDITED BY JANE ADAMS
INTRODUCED BY JILLIAN STEWART
DESIGNED BY PHILIP CLUCAS
FOOD PHOTOGRAPHY BY PETER BARRY

MALLARD PRESS

An imprint of BDD Promotional Book Company, Inc.,
666 Fifth Avenue, New York, N.Y. 10103.
Mallard Press and its accompanying design and logo
are trademarks of BDD Promotional Book Company, Inc.

CLB 2372
Copyright © 1990 Colour Library Books Ltd.,
Godalming, Surrey, England.
Text filmsetting by Words and Spaces, Hampshire England.
First published in the United States of America
in 1990 by the Mallard Press.
Printed and bound in Hong Kong.
All rights reserved
ISBN 0 792 45226 7

AMERICA
AND ITS
CUISINE

MALLARD
PRESS

CONTENTS

Title page: Braised Rabbit with Peppers.
Previous pages: Cranberry Orange Sauce.
These pages: a dusky sunset over Harris Beach
State Park in Oregon.

INTRODUCTION

Historically, American cuisine is rich and varied, so it is unfortunate that it seems to have become stuck with a reputation for "fast food," gigantic steaks and fattening cakes, all of which belies the wealth of available recipes both old and new. Although the popularity of these recipes is widespread, many Americans still tend to look abroad for culinary inspiration, believing their own home-grown cookery to be uninspiring and unhealthful.

In rediscovering true American cooking, you will realize there is no reason to be envious of, say, French or Italian cuisines for their distinctive flavors when we have a combination of the best of these and many other cuisines. The first immigrants brought to their adopted land the best of their own home cooking from as far afield as the Far East and Western Europe. Consequently American cooking is incredibly rich in variety and in flavors. How could it be otherwise with such a rich diversity of cultural influences? *America and its Cuisine* features some of the best recipes from all over the United States, combining the classic and the new in a delicious selection which invites you to explore our culinary heritage and development.

The history of America and its cuisine are intertwined. Much is made of America as a melting pot and nowhere is this more evident than in the amalgamation of cuisines that make up American cooking. It is based on a foundation of local knowledge from the Indians. Successive generations of immigrants then brought with them their own recipes and methods of cooking and adapted them to the conditions they found in their adopted homeland. The first immigrants faced great hardship and near starvation in the early years, and were forced to rely on native crops and the guidance of the Indians, who introduced them to maize, squash, and pumpkin. Wild game was plentiful and, once caught, provided an excellent source of food. The Indians also introduced the settlers to domesticated turkeys, little realizing their future significance in the traditional Thanksgiving dinner.

As well as this American classic, many more of those earliest recipes are still popular today. New England provided the first settlers with a wealth of fish and seafood, and, as a great percentage of today's population still live near an ocean or lake, the prominence of fish and seafood in the American diet has continued to this day.

As the population extended its boundaries so the influence of the land became more evident. Different climatic and crop conditions gave rise to different recipes. Right across the United States the variety and richness of our cuisine is as stunning as the landscape. Its geographical diversity has resulted in a gold mine of widely differing recipes.

From the southwest, for example, come the spicy hot flavors of Tex-Mex food. In marked contrast, the food of New England is much more conservative, reflecting those states' close ties with the Pilgrim Fathers and the many other English settlers who colonized the area. Californian food takes us to the other side of the country with a culinary style that is bang up to date; a truly cosmopolitan blend of all that has gone before, transformed with a touch of Californian imagination. In between these three styles of cooking, are many others, which you will find represented within these pages. With clearly written, easy-to-follow recipes and many color photographs to tempt you, your culinary journey through the cuisine of America should be both exciting and delicious.

Arizona (facing page) is a state of harsh yet awesome beauty, its landscapes shaped by erosion and glowing with intense color.

Serves 4
Cornmeal Pancakes

Cornmeal, either yellow, white or blue, is an important ingredient in Tex-Mex recipes. Here it's combined with corn in a light and different kind of appetizer.

PREPARATION TIME: 30 minutes
COOKING TIME: 3-4 minutes per pancake

---

1 cup yellow cornmeal
1 tbsp flour
1 tsp baking soda
1 tsp salt
2 cups buttermilk
2 eggs, separated

Oil
10oz frozen corn
Sour cream
Red pepper preserves
Green onions, chopped

Sift the dry ingredients into a bowl, adding any coarse meal that remains in the strainer. Mix the egg yolks and buttermilk together and gradually beat into the dry ingredients. Cover and leave to stand for at least 15 minutes. Whip the egg whites until stiff but not dry and fold into the cornmeal mixture.

Lightly grease a frying pan with oil and drop in about 2 tbsps of batter. Sprinkle with the corn and allow to cook until the underside is golden brown. Turn the pancakes and cook the second side until golden. Continue with the remaining batter and corn. Keep the cooked pancakes warm.

To serve, place three pancakes on warm side plates. Add a spoonful of sour cream and red pepper preserves to each and sprinkle over finely sliced or shredded green onions.

Facing page: a meadow overflowing with Indian Paintbrush and Bluebonnets, the official state flower of Texas.

SERVES 8-10

Red Bean and Red Pepper Soup

Red beans are very popular in southern Louisiana, and here they make a hearty soup when combined with red peppers and red wine.

PREPARATION TIME: 25 minutes plus overnight soaking
COOKING TIME: 3 hours

1lb dried red kidney beans
Water to cover
2 onions, coarsely chopped
3 sticks celery, coarsely chopped
2 bay leaves
Salt and pepper

3 large red peppers, seeded and
    finely chopped
4 tbsps red wine
10 cups chicken stock
Lemon wedges and 4 chopped
    hard-boiled eggs to garnish

Soak the beans in the water overnight. Alternatively, bring them to the boil and boil rapidly for 2 minutes. Leave to stand for 1 hour.

Drain off the liquid and add the onions, celery, bay leaves, salt and pepper, red peppers, red wine and stock. Bring to the boil over high heat, stirring occasionally. Reduce the heat and allow to simmer, partially covered, for about 3 hours, or until the beans are completely tender.

Remove the bay leaves and purée the soup in a food processor or blender. Serve garnished with the chopped hard-boiled egg. Serve the lemon wedges on the side.

In the days when New Orleans was a cotton port, steamers plied the waters of the Mississippi.
The stern-wheeler Natchez *is the ninth of that name and is still working as a pleasure boat.*

SERVES 6-8

Cioppino

California's famous and delicious fish stew is Italian in heritage, but a close relative of French Bouillabaisse, too.

PREPARATION TIME: 40 minutes
COOKING TIME: 40 minutes

1lb spinach, well washed
1 tbsp each chopped fresh basil, thyme, rosemary and sage
2 tbsps chopped fresh marjoram
4 tbsps chopped parsley
1 large red pepper, seeded and finely chopped
2 cloves garlic, crushed
24 large fresh clams or 48 mussels, well scrubbed
1 large crab, cooked

1lb monkfish or rock salmon (huss)
12 large shrimp, cooked and unpeeled
1lb canned plum tomatoes and juice
2 tbsps tomato paste
4 tbsps olive oil
Pinch salt and pepper
½-1 cup dry white wine
Water

Chop the spinach leaves roughly after removing any tough stems. Combine the spinach with the herbs, chopped red pepper and garlic, and set aside.

Discard any clams or mussels with broken shells or ones that do not close when tapped. Place the shellfish in the bottom of a large pot and sprinkle over a layer of the spinach mixture.

Break the claws of the crab, crack slightly and reserve. Turn the crab over and press up with the thumbs to separate the body from the shell. Discard the stomach sac and lungs (dead-man's fingers). Pick out the white meat from the body and scrape out the brown meat from the shell. Place the crab on top of the spinach and then add another spinach layer.

Add the fish and a spinach layer, followed by the shrimp and any remaining spinach.

Mix the tomatoes, tomato paste, oil, wine and seasonings and pour over the seafood and spinach. Cover the pot and simmer the mixture for about 40 minutes. If more liquid is necessary, add water. Spoon into soup bowls, dividing the fish and shellfish evenly.

The sun rises to reveal the early morning quiet of Malibu Beach, California.

SERVES 6

Seafood Pan Roast

This mixture of oysters and crab is a descendant of French gratin recipes
and makes a delicious, but substantial, appetizer.

PREPARATION TIME: 40 minutes
COOKING TIME: 30 minutes

---

24 small oysters on the half shell
1 cup fish stock
1 cup light cream
1 large or 2 small cooked crabs
4 slices bread, crusts trimmed and
    made into crumbs
⅓ cup butter or margarine

6 tbsps flour
1 bunch green onions, chopped
2oz parsley, chopped
2 tbsps Worcestershire sauce
½ tsp tabasco
Pinch salt

Remove the oysters from their shells with a small, sharp knife. Place the oysters in a
saucepan and strain over any oyster liquid. Add the fish stock and cook gently until
the oysters curl around the edges. Remove the oysters, keep them warm and strain the
liquid into a clean pan. Add the cream to the oyster liquid and bring to the boil. Allow
to boil rapidly for about 5 minutes.

    Remove the crab claws and legs. Turn the crabs over and push out the body with
your thumbs. Remove the stomach sac and lungs (dead man's fingers) and discard. Cut
the body in four sections with a large, sharp knife and pick out the meat with a skewer.
Crack the claws and legs to extract the meat. Leave the small legs whole for garnish, if
desired. Scrape out the brown meat from inside the shell and combine it with the
breadcrumbs and white meat from the body and claws.

    Melt the butter or margarine in a medium-sized saucepan and stir in the flour. Cook
gently for 5 minutes. Add the onions and parsley and cook a further 5 minutes. Pour
over the cream and fish stock mixture, stirring constantly. Add the Worcestershire
sauce, tabasco and salt, and cook about 15-20 minutes over low heat, stirring
occasionally. Fold in the crab meat and breadcrumb mixture.

    Place the oysters in the bottom of a buttered casserole or in individual dishes and
spoon the crab meat mixture on top. Broil to brown, if desired, and serve immediately.

*Facing page: the clear waters of Little Missouri Falls in the
Arkansas Ozarks.*

SERVES 4

Eggs Sardou

A traditional New Orleans brunch dish, this makes a substantial appetizer
or even a light supper dish.

PREPARATION TIME: 45 minutes
COOKING TIME: 15-21 minutes, in total

1½lbs fresh spinach
1½ tbsps butter or margarine
1 tbsp flour
1 cup milk
Salt, pepper and nutmeg
4 artichoke hearts, quartered
4 eggs

HOLLANDAISE SAUCE
3 egg yolks
⅔ cup unsalted butter
1 tbsp lemon juice
Pinch salt and pepper
1 large piece canned pimento,
    drained and cut into thin strips

Strip the spinach leaves from the stalks and wash the leaves well. Place the leaves in a
large saucepan and add a pinch of salt. Cover the pan and cook the spinach over
moderate heat in only the water that clings to the leaves. When the spinach is just
wilted, take off the heat and drain well. Chop roughly and set aside.

    Melt the butter or margarine in a medium-sized saucepan and stir in the flour.
Gradually add the milk, beating constantly, and place the sauce over low heat. Beat
the sauce as it comes to the boil and allow it to boil rapidly for about one minute to
thicken. Stir in the spinach and season the sauce with salt, pepper and nutmeg. Add
the artichoke hearts and set the sauce aside.

*Trees on the slopes of the Great Smoky Mountains are a haze of
green and gold, signalling the arrival of fall.*

Fill a large sauté pan with water and bring to the boil. Turn down the heat and, when the water is just barely simmering, break an egg into a cup or onto a saucer. Gently lower the egg into the water to poach. Repeat with the remaining eggs. Poach over a gentle heat, never allowing the water to boil. Alternatively, cook in a special poaching pan. Cook until the whites have set but the yolks are still soft. Remove the eggs from the pan with a draining spoon and place in cold water until ready to use.

Place the egg yolks in a food processor or blender with the lemon juice and seasoning. Process once or twice to mix. Place the butter in a small saucepan and melt over gentle heat. Turn up the heat and when the butter is bubbling, take off the heat. With the machine running, gradually pour the butter onto the eggs in a very thin but steady stream.

To assemble the dish, reheat the spinach sauce and place an equal amount of it on each plate. Make a well in center. Place the eggs back into hot water briefly to reheat, and drain well. Place an egg in the hollow of the spinach sauce on each plate. Spoon over some of the Hollandaise sauce to coat each egg completely. Make a cross with two strips of pimento on top of each egg and serve immediately.

SERVES 6

Zucchini Slippers

Italian immigrants to California popularized the zucchini, which is used
here to make an original appetizer.

PREPARATION TIME: 30 minutes
COOKING TIME: 23-25 minutes

---

6 even-sized zucchini
½ cup cottage cheese, drained
1 cup grated Colby cheese
1 small red pepper, seeded and
   chopped

2 tbsps chopped parsley
Pinch salt and cayenne pepper
1 large egg
Watercress or parsley, to garnish

Trim the ends of the zucchini and cook in boiling salted water for about 8 minutes, or
steam for 10 minutes. Remove from the water or steamer and cut in half. Allow to cool
slightly and then scoop out the center, leaving a narrow margin of flesh on the skin to
form a shell. Invert each zucchini slipper onto a paper towel to drain, reserving the
scooped-out flesh.

    Chop the flesh and mix with the remaining ingredients. Spoon filling into the shells
and arrange in a greased baking pan. Bake, uncovered, in a preheated 350°F oven for
15 minutes. Broil, if desired, to brown the top. Garnish with watercress or parsley.

*Facing page: the breathtaking waterfalls and towering peaks of
Yosemite National Park in California.*

SERVES 4

Peanut Soup

Peanuts, popular all over the South, make a velvety rich soup that is easily
made from ordinary store cupboard ingredients

PREPARATION TIME: 15 minutes
COOKING TIME: 15 minutes

4 tbsps butter or margarine
2 tbsps flour
1 cup creamy peanut butter
¼ tsp celery seed

2½ cups chicken stock
½ cup dry sherry
½ cup coarsely chopped peanuts

Melt the butter or margarine in a medium-sized saucepan. Remove from the heat and
stir in the flour. Add the peanut butter and celery seed. Gradually pour on the stock,
stirring constantly.

Return the pan to the heat and simmer gently for about 15 minutes. Do not allow to
boil rapidly. Stir in the sherry and ladle into a tureen or individual bowls. Sprinkle
with the chopped peanuts.

Top: Lake Chalague, Hiawasee, Georgia. Above left: swamplands near the tobacco-producing city of Tifton, Georgia. Above right: the 90-foot-high and 190-foot-wide Stone Mountain Carving, Georgia.

SERVES 6-8

Cream of Pumpkin Soup

Pumpkins have an honoured place in American culinary history and show
up in many different preparations. Their excellent color and texture make
a distinctive soup.

PREPARATION TIME: 45 minutes
COOKING TIME: 20 minutes

---

1 large pumpkin about 4-5lbs in
  weight
¼ cup butter or margarine
1 large onion, sliced

1 cup heavy cream
Pinch salt, white pepper and
  nutmeg
Snipped chives to garnish

Wash the pumpkin well on the outside and slice off the top about 2 inches down from
the stem end. Carefully cut most of the pulp from the top and reserve the "lid" for later
use. Remove the seeds from the inside and discard them. Using a small, sharp knife,
carefully remove all but ½ inch of the pulp from inside the pumpkin. Work slowly and
carefully to avoid piercing the outer skin of the pumpkin. Chop all the pulp from the
top and the inside of the pumpkin and set it aside.

  Melt the butter or margarine in a large saucepan and add the onion. Cook slowly
until the onion is tender but not brown. Add the pumpkin flesh and about 4 cups cold
water. Bring to the boil and then allow to simmer gently, covered, for about 20
minutes. Purée the mixture in a food processor or blender in several small batches.
Return the soup to the pot and add the cream, salt, pepper and nutmeg to taste.
Reheat the soup and pour it into the reserved pumpkin shell. Garnish the top of the
soup with snipped chives, if desired, before serving. Bring to the table, covered with
the pumpkin "lid".

The figure seated on a rock in the foreground gives some idea of the immense size of Capitol Gorge, Capitol Reef National Park.

SERVES 4

Trout with Chorizo

For fish with a spicy difference, try this as a dinner party dish to impress
and please your fish-loving friends.

PREPARATION TIME: 25 minutes
COOKING TIME: 35 minutes, in total

1 boned trout (about 2lbs in boned
   weight)
8oz chorizo or other spicy sausage
Water
1 small green pepper, seeded and
   finely chopped
2 small onions, finely chopped
1 slice bread, made into crumbs

4 tbsps dry white wine
Lemon juice
½ cup natural yogurt
1 tsp garlic powder
2 tsps chopped fresh coriander
   leaves
Salt and pepper

Have the fishmonger bone the trout, leaving the head and tail on the fish.

Place the chorizo in a pan and cover with water. Bring to the boil and then cook for
10 minutes to soften and to remove excess fat. Skin the sausage and chop the meat
finely. Combine with the green pepper, onion, breadcrumbs and wine.

Sprinkle the fish cavity with the lemon juice. Stuff the fish with the sausage mixture
and place on lightly-oiled aluminum foil. Seal the ends to form a parcel and bake in a
preheated 350°F oven for about 20-30 minutes, or until the fish feels firm and the
flesh looks opaque.

Combine the yogurt, garlic powder, chopped coriander and seasonings to taste.
Remove the fish from the foil and transfer to a serving plate. Spoon some of the sauce
over the fish and serve the rest separately.

*Alaska, one of America's last great wildernesses, is a mysterious
and charismatic land of immense open spaces and stunning
scenery.*

SERVES 6

Seafood Gumbo Filé

Either filé powder, made from sassafras leaves, or okra gives a Cajun gumbo its characteristic texture. Gumbos are good without filé, too.

PREPARATION TIME: 25-30 minutes
COOKING TIME: 20-25 minutes

1lb cooked, unpeeled shrimp
2 dried red chili peppers, crumbled
½ tbsp each whole cloves, whole allspice, coriander and mustard seeds and dill weed
1 tsp celery seed
5 cups water
4 tbsps butter or margarine
1 onion, peeled and sliced
1 green pepper, seeded and sliced
2 cloves garlic, finely chopped

3 tbsps flour
½ tsp thyme
1 bay leaf
2 tbsps chopped parsley
Dash Worcestershire sauce
12 oysters, shelled
8oz tomatoes, peeled and chopped
2 tbsps filé powder (optional)
Salt and pepper
Cooked rice

Peel the shrimp and reserve the shells. Mix shells with the spice mixture and water and bring to the boil in a large stock pot. Reduce the heat and allow to simmer for about 20 minutes.

Melt the butter or margarine and, when foaming, add the onion, green pepper, garlic and flour. Cook slowly, stirring constantly, until the flour is a pale golden brown. Gradually strain on the stock, discarding the shells and spice mixture. Add the thyme and bay leaf and stir well. Bring to the boil and then simmer until thick.

Add the parsley and the Worcestershire sauce to taste. Add the oysters, peeled shrimp and tomatoes and heat through gently to cook the oysters. Stir in the filé powder and leave to stand to thicken. Adjust the seasoning and serve over rice.

Above: the breathtaking view from the top of Petit Jean Mountain, Arkansas.

Top: Seafood Gumbo Filé. Above left: Round Springs State Park, Missouri. Above right: Moon Lake, north of Friars Point, Coahoma County, Mississippi.

SERVES 4

Swordfish with Grapefruit Tequila Salsa

Rich and dense in texture, swordfish takes very well to a tart grapefruit accompaniment with a dash of tequila.

PREPARATION TIME: 35 minutes
COOKING TIME: 8 minutes

4-6 ruby or pink grapefruit
   (depending on size)
1 lime
Half a green chili, seeded and
   finely diced
1 green onion, finely chopped
2 tbsps chopped fresh coriander
1 tbsp sugar

3 tbsps tequila
4-8 swordfish steaks (depending
   on size)
Juice of 1 extra lime
2 tbsps oil
Black pepper to taste
Coriander sprigs for garnish

Remove the zest from the grapefruit and lime with a zester and set it aside. Remove all the pith from the grapefruit and segment them. Squeeze the lime for juice. Mix the grapefruit and citrus zests with the chili, onion, coriander, sugar, tequila and lime juice and set aside.

Mix the extra lime juice, oil and pepper together and brush both sides of the fish. Place under a preheated broiler and cook for about 4 minutes each side depending on distance from the heat source.

To serve, place a coriander sprig on each fish steak and serve with the grapefruit salsa.

Facing page: Maroon Lake near Aspen, Colorado.

SERVES 4

Snapper with Fennel and Orange Salad

Red snapper brings Florida to mind. Combined with that state's oranges, it makes a lovely summer meal.

PREPARATION TIME: 30 minutes
COOKING TIME: 6-10 minutes

4 even-sized red snapper, cleaned, heads and tails on	2 bulbs fennel
Oil	2 oranges
Juice of 1 lemon	3 tbsps light salad oil
	Pinch sugar, salt and black pepper

Brush both sides of the fish with oil and cut three slits in the sides of each. Sprinkle with a little of the lemon juice, reserving the rest.

Slice the fennel in half and remove the cores. Slice thinly. Also slice the green tops and chop the feathery herb to use in the dressing. Peel the oranges, removing all the white pith. Cut the oranges into segments. Do this over a bowl to catch the juice.

Add the remaining lemon juice to any orange juice collected in the bowl. Add the oil, salt, pepper and a pinch of sugar, if necessary. Mix well and add the fennel, green herb tops and orange segments, stirring carefully.

Broil the fish 3-5 minutes per side, depending on thickness. Serve the fish with the heads and tails on, accompanied by the salad.

The cosmopolitan atmosphere of Miami has ensured its continuing development and popularity as a holiday resort.

SERVES 4

Boston Scrod

Scrod, or baby codfish, provides the perfect base for a crunchy, slightly spicy topping. Boston is justly famous for it.

PREPARATION TIME: 15 minutes
COOKING TIME: 10-12 minutes

---

4 even-sized cod fillets	1 tsp onion salt
Salt and pepper	Dash Worcestershire sauce and
⅓ cup butter, melted	tabasco
¾ cup dry bread crumbs	2 tbsps lemon juice
1 tsp dry mustard	1 tbsp finely chopped parsley

Season the fish fillets with salt and pepper and place them on a broiler tray. Brush with a little of the melted butter and broil for about 5 minutes.

Combine the remaining butter with the bread crumbs, mustard, onion salt, Worcestershire sauce, tabasco, lemon juice and parsley. Spoon the mixture carefully on top of each fish fillet, covering it completely. Press down lightly to pack the crumbs into place. Broil for a further 5-7 minutes, or until the top is lightly browned and the fish flakes.

Many visitors are attracted each year to the long, sandy shores of Cape Cod, yet is is always possible to find a quiet spot away from the crowds.

SERVES 4

Oysters Rockefeller

Oysters can be purchased already opened, and you'll find the rest of this famous New Orleans dish simplicity itself to prepare.

PREPARATION TIME: 25 minutes
COOKING TIME: 25 minutes

---

24 oysters on the half shell
Rock salt
6 strips bacon, finely chopped
1¼lbs fresh spinach, well washed, stems removed and leaves finely chopped
1 small bunch green onions, finely chopped

2 cloves garlic, crushed
4-5 tbsps fine fresh bread crumbs
Dash tabasco
2 tbsps aniseed liqueur
Pinch salt
Parmesan cheese

Loosen the oysters from their shells, strain and reserve their liquid. Rinse the shells well and return an oyster to each one. Pour about 1 inch of rock salt into a baking pan and place in the oysters in their shells, pressing each shell gently into the salt.

Place the bacon in a large frying pan and cook slowly to render the fat. Turn up the heat and brown the bacon evenly. Add the spinach, green onions and garlic and cook slowly until softened. Add the breadcrumbs, tabasco, oyster liquid, liqueur, and a pinch of salt.

Spoon some of the mixture onto each oyster and sprinkle with Parmesan cheese. Place in a preheated 350°F oven for about 15 minutes. Alternatively, heat through in the oven for 10 minutes and place under a preheated broiler to lightly brown the cheese. Serve immediately.

The thirty-four-story Louisiana State Capitol Building rises above
the lush vegetation in Baton Rouge, Louisiana.

Serves 2

Barbecued Shrimp

It's the sauce rather than the cooking method that gives this dish its name.
It's spicy, zippy and *hot*.

PREPARATION TIME: 15 minutes
COOKING TIME: 5 minutes

1lb large shrimp, cooked and
    unpeeled
½ cup unsalted butter
1 tsp each white, black and
    cayenne pepper
1 tsp each chopped fresh thyme,
    rosemary and marjoram

1 clove garlic, crushed
1 tsp Worcestershire sauce
½ cup fish stock
4 tbsps dry white wine
Salt
Cooked rice

Remove the eyes and the legs from the shrimp.

Melt the butter in a large frying pan and add the white pepper, black pepper, cayenne pepper, herbs and garlic. Add the shrimp and toss over heat for a few minutes. Remove the shrimp and set them aside. Add the Worcestershire sauce, stock and wine to the ingredients in the pan. Bring to the boil and cook for about 3 minutes to reduce. Add salt to taste.

Arrange the shrimp on a bed of rice and pour over the sauce to serve.

*A perfectly blue sky is reflected in the still waters of Lake
Washington, Washington County.*

SERVES 4

Crawfish Pie

This seafood, plentiful in southern Louisiana, is used in many delicious ways. The boiling mixture adds spice, and the browned flour a nutty taste and good color.

PREPARATION TIME: 30 minutes
COOKING TIME: 35 minutes

PASTRY
2 cups all-purpose flour, sifted
Pinch salt
½-¾ cup butter or margarine
Cold water
2 dried red chili peppers, crumbled
½ tbsp each whole cloves, whole allspice, coriander seed and mustard seed
½ tbsp dill weed, fresh or dried
1 tbsp celery seed
1lb raw crawfish or shrimp

FILLING
3 tbsps oil
3 tbsps flour
½ green pepper, seeded and finely diced
2 green onions, finely chopped
1 stick celery, finely chopped
1 cup light cream
Salt and pepper

Sift the flour into a bowl with a pinch of salt and rub in the butter or margarine until the mixture resembles fine breadcrumbs. Add enough cold water to bring the mixture together. Knead into a ball, wrap well and chill for about 30 minutes before use.

Combine the spices with about 2½ cups water. Bring to the boil and add the crawfish or shrimp. Cook for about 5 minutes, stirring occasionally, until the shellfish curl up. Remove from the liquid and leave to drain.

Heat the oil for the filling in a small saucepan and add the flour. Cook slowly, stirring constantly, until the flour turns a rich dark brown. Add the remaining filling ingredients, stirring constantly while adding the cream. Bring to the boil, reduce the heat and cook for about 5 minutes. Add the crawfish or shrimp to the sauce.

Divide the pastry into 4 and roll out each portion on a lightly-floured surface to about ¼ inch thick. Line individual flan or pie dishes with the pastry, pushing it carefully onto the base and down the sides, taking care not to stretch it. Trim off excess pastry and reserve. Place a sheet of wax paper or foil on the pastry and pour in rice, pasta or baking beans to come halfway up the sides. Bake the pastry blind for about 10 minutes in a preheated 400°F oven. Remove the paper and beans for an additional 5 minutes to cook the base.

Spoon in the filling and roll out any trimmings to make a lattice pattern on top. Bake a further 10 minutes to brown the lattice and heat the filling. Cool slightly before serving.

New Orleans' famous Mardi Gras celebrations bring thousands of people onto the streets to marvel at the extravagantly ornate floats.

SERVES 4

Fried Bass in Cornmeal

As a coating for frying, cornmeal is superb. It fries to a crisp crunch and
adds a subtle flavor of its own.

PREPARATION TIME: 20 minutes
COOKING TIME: 5 minutes per batch

---

2 cups yellow cornmeal
2 tbsps flour
Pinch salt
2 tsps cayenne pepper
1 tsp ground cumin

2 tsps garlic granules
2lbs freshwater bass or other
   whitefish fillets
Milk
Lime wedges to garnish

Mix the cornmeal, flour, salt, cayenne, cumin and garlic together in a shallow
container or on a piece of wax paper.

Skin the fillets if desired. Dip them into the milk and then lift to allow the excess to
drip off. Place the fish in the cornmeal mixture and turn with two forks or, if using
paper, lift the ends and toss the fish to coat.

Meanwhile, heat oil in a deep frying pan, large saucepan or deep-fat fryer. Add the
fish in small batches and cook until the fillets float to the surface. Turn over and cook
to brown lightly and evenly.

Drain on paper towels and serve immediately with lime wedges.

*A harbor in Rhode Island, New England, bears witness to the fact
that fishing still plays a crucial part in the local economy.*

SERVES 4

Spiced Lamb

French influence is evident in this dish, but so is the Creole, with a good pinch of allspice and bright red peppers.

PREPARATION TIME: 25 minutes
MARINATING TIME: 4 hours
COOKING TIME: 35 minutes

1lb lamb neck fillet
1 tsp fresh dill, chopped
1 tsp rosemary, crushed
1 tsp thyme, chopped
2 tsp mustard seeds, crushed
   slightly
2 bay leaves
1 tsp coarsely ground black pepper
½ tsp ground allspice
Juice of 2 lemons

1 cup red wine
2 tbsps oil
1 small red pepper, seeded and
   sliced
3oz button mushrooms, left whole
2 tbsps butter or margarine
3 tbsps flour
½ cup beef stock
Salt

Place the lamb in a shallow dish and sprinkle on the dill, rosemary, thyme and mustard seeds. Add the bay leaves, pepper, allspice, lemon juice and wine, and stir to coat the meat thoroughly with the marinade. Leave for 4 hours in the refrigerator.

Heat the oil in a large frying pan and add the red pepper and mushrooms and cook to soften slightly. Remove with a draining spoon. Reheat the oil in the pan and add the lamb fillet, well drained and patted dry. Reserve the marinade. Brown the meat quickly on all sides to seal. Remove from the pan and set aside with the vegetables.

Melt the butter in the pan and when foaming add the flour. Lower the heat and cook the flour slowly until it is a good, rich brown. Pour in the beef stock and the marinade. Bring to the boil and return the vegetables and lamb to the pan. Cook about 15 minutes, or until the lamb is tender, but still pink inside. Slice the lamb fillet thinly on the diagonal and arrange on individual plates. Remove the bay leaves and spoon the sauce over the meat to serve.

St. Louis's famous Gateway Arch provides a stunning panorama of the city from its observation tower.

SERVES 6-8

Chili Roja

Red meat, red onions, red peppers, paprika, tomatoes and red beans all give clues to the name of this zesty Tex-Mex stew.

PREPARATION TIME: 25 minutes
COOKING TIME: 1½-2 hours

Oil
2lbs beef chuck, cut into 1-inch
    pieces
1 large red onion, coarsely
    chopped
2 cloves garlic, crushed
2 red peppers, seeded and cut into
    1-inch pieces
1-2 red chilies, seeded and finely
    chopped
3 tbsps mild chili powder
1 tbsp cumin

1 tbsp paprika
3 cups beer, water or stock
8oz canned tomatoes, puréed
2 tbsps tomato paste
8oz canned red kidney beans,
    drained
Pinch salt
6 ripe tomatoes, peeled, seeded
    and diced

Pour about 4 tbsps oil into a large saucepan or flameproof casserole. When hot, brown the meat in small batches over a moderately high heat for about 5 minutes per batch.

Set aside the meat on a plate or in the lid of the casserole. Lower the heat and cook the onion, garlic, red peppers and chilies for about 5 minutes. Add the chili powder, cumin and paprika and cook for 1 minute further. Pour over the liquid and add the canned tomatoes, tomato paste and the meat. Cook slowly for about 1½-2 hours. Add the beans about 45 minutes before the end of cooking time.

When the meat is completely tender, add salt to taste and serve garnished with the diced tomatoes.

The Fort Union National Monument preserves the ruins of a historic fort that once protected travelers on the nearby Santa Fe Trail.

SERVES 4-6

Barbecued Spareribs

This Chinese-style barbecue sauce makes a delicious change from the usual tomato-based one, so give your next barbecue a hint of Oriental glamor.

PREPARATION TIME: 45 minutes, plus 1 hour marinating time
COOKING TIME: 1 hour

4lbs fresh spareribs
3 tbsps dark soy sauce
6 tbsps hoisin sauce

2 tbsps dry sherry
¼ tsp five-spice powder
1 tbsp brown sugar

Cut the spareribs into one-rib pieces. Mix all the remaining ingredients together, pour over the ribs and stir to coat evenly. Allow to stand for 1 hour.

Put the sparerib pieces on a rack in a roasting pan containing 2 cups water and cook in a preheated 350°F oven for 30 minutes. Add more hot water to the pan while cooking, if necessary.

Turn the ribs over and brush with the remaining sauce. Cook 30 minutes longer, or until tender.

The marinated spareribs can also be cooked over a barbecue.

Facing page: sunset in the Ala Moana Park, Hawaii, a favorite recreation area for both locals and tourists.

SERVES 6-8

Yankee Pot Roast

This classic American recipe has its roots in French and German cuisine.
It is an excellent way with economical cuts of beef.

PREPARATION TIME: 30 minutes
COOKING TIME: 2-2½ hours

3lb beef roast (rump, chuck, round
    or top end)
Flour seasoned with salt and
    pepper
2 tbsps butter or margarine
1 onion stuck with 2 cloves
1 bay leaf
2 tsps fresh thyme or 1 tsp dried
    thyme

1 cup beef stock
4 carrots
12 small onions, peeled
4 small turnips, peeled and left
    whole
2 potatoes, cut into even-sized
    pieces
2 tbsps butter or margarine mixed
    with 2 tbsps flour

Dredge the beef with the seasoned flour, patting off the excess. Melt the butter in a large, heavy-based casserole or saucepan and, when foaming, brown the meat on all sides, turning it with wooden spoons or a spatula. When well browned, add the onion stuck with the cloves, bay leaf and thyme and pour on the stock. Cover the pan, reduce the heat and cook on top of the stove or in a preheated 300°F oven. Cook slowly for about 2 hours, adding more liquid, either stock or water, as necessary.

Test the meat and, if beginning to feel tender, add the vegetables. Cover and continue to cook until the meat is completely tender and the vegetables are cooked through. Remove the meat and vegetables from the casserole or pan and place them on a warm serving platter. Skim the excess fat from the top of the sauce and bring it back to the boil.

Mix the butter and flour (beurre manié) to a smooth paste. Add about 1 tsp of the mixture to the boiling sauce and beat thoroughly. Continue adding the mixture until the sauce is of the desired thickness. Carve the meat and spoon over some of the sauce. Serve the rest of the sauce separately.

*The sun sinks slowly over the farmlands of Delaware, creating
dramatic silhouettes and fiery cloudscapes.*

SERVES 4

Panéed Lemon Veal

Panéed means pan-fried in Creole – a perfect way to prepare this tender cut of veal that only needs brief cooking.

PREPARATION TIME: 25 minutes
COOKING TIME: 20-25 minutes

8 veal cutlets
Flour for dredging
Salt and pepper
2 tbsps butter or margarine
1 green pepper, seeded and thinly
   sliced

6 tbsps dry white wine
1 tbsp lemon juice
¾ cup chicken stock
1 lemon, peeled and thinly sliced

Dredge the veal with a mixture of flour, salt and pepper. Shake off the excess. Melt the butter or margarine in a large frying pan or sauté pan and brown the veal, a few pieces at a time. Remove the meat and keep it warm. Cook the peppers briefly and set aside with the veal. Pour the wine and lemon juice into the pan to deglaze. Add the stock and bring to the boil. Boil for 5 minutes to reduce. Add the veal and peppers and cook 15 minutes over gentle heat. Add the lemons and heat through before serving.

Shenandoah Farm typifies the quiet rural life of West Virginia.

SERVES 8-10

Alabama Cola Glazed Ham

Don't be afraid to try this somewhat unusual approach to roast ham. Cola gives it a marvelous taste and color.

PREPARATION TIME: 30 minutes, plus overnight soaking
COOKING TIME: 2¼ hours

10lb joint country or Smithfield
   ham
4 cups cola soft drink

Whole cloves
1 cup packed dark brown sugar

Soak the ham overnight.

Preheat oven to 350°F. Place the ham rind side down in a roasting pan. Pour over all but 6 tbsps of the cola and bake, uncovered, 1½ hours or until the internal temperature registers 140°F. Baste the ham every 20 minutes with the pan juices, using a large spoon or a bulb baster.

Remove the ham from the oven and allow it to cool for 10-15 minutes. Remove the rind from the ham with a small, sharp knife and score the fat to a depth of ¼ inch in a criss-cross pattern. Stick 1 clove in the center of every other diamond. Mix the sugar and the remaining cola together and pour or spread over the ham. Raise the oven temperature to 375°F.

Return the ham to the oven and bake for 45 minutes, basting every 15 minutes. Cover loosely with aluminum foil if the ham begins to brown too much. Allow to stand 15 minutes before slicing.

Calm waters reflect a colorful sunset near Fort Morgan, Alabama.

Top: the jade green of the Colorado River stands out against the
Grand Canyon. Above left: the Sangre de Cristo Mountains in New
Mexico. Above right: Scotts Bluff National Monument, Nebraska.

SERVES 4

Spareribs in Chili & Cream Sauce

Unsweetened cocoa lends color and depth to a sauce for ribs that brings sophistication to Tex-Mex cooking.

PREPARATION TIME: 20 minutes
COOKING TIME: 50-55 minutes

2¼lbs spareribs
1 tsp unsweetened cocoa
1 tbsp flour
½ tsp cumin
½ tsp paprika
½ tsp dried oregano, crushed

Salt and pepper
1 cup warm water
2 tbsps thin honey
2 tbsps heavy cream
Lime wedges, to garnish

Leave the ribs in whole slabs and roast at 400°F for 20-25 minutes, or until well browned. Drain off all the excess fat.

Blend together the cocoa, flour, cumin, paprika, oregano, seasoning, water and honey and pour over the ribs. Lower the temperature to 350°F and cook ribs for a further 30 minutes, until the sauce has reduced and the ribs are tender.

Cut the ribs into pieces and arrange on a serving dish. Pour the cream into the sauce in the roasting pan and place over moderate heat. Bring to the boil and pour over the ribs. Garnish with lime wedges and serve.

SERVES 6

Sweet Potato and Sausage Casserole

This close relative of the French soufflé is easier to make, and includes two great favorites – sweet potatoes and sausage.

PREPARATION TIME: 35 minutes
COOKING TIME: 45 minutes

2lbs sweet potatoes
2 tbsps oil
8oz sausage meat
1 small onion, finely chopped
2 sticks celery, finely chopped

½ green pepper, finely chopped
Pinch sage and thyme
Pinch salt and pepper
2 eggs, separated

Peel the sweet potatoes and cut them into 2-inch pieces. Place in boiling water to cover and add a pinch of salt. Cook quickly, uncovered, for about 20 minutes or until the sweet potatoes are tender to the point of a knife. Drain them well and leave them to dry. Purée the potatoes using a potato masher.

While the potatoes are cooking, heat the oil in a large frying pan and add the sausage meat. Cook briskly, breaking up with a fork until the meat is golden brown. Add the onion, celery and green pepper, and cook for a further 5 minutes. Add the sage, thyme and a pinch of seasoning.

Beat the egg yolks into the mashed sweet potatoes and, using an electric mixer or a hand whisk, beat the egg whites until stiff but not dry. Drain any excess fat from the sausage meat and combine it with the sweet potatoes. Fold in the whisked egg whites until thoroughly incorporated. Spoon the mixture into a well-buttered casserole dish or soufflé dish and bake in a preheated 375°F oven, until well risen and brown on the top, about 25–30 minutes. Serve immediately.

Cattle ranching still has an important role in many communities in Arkansas.

SERVES 4

Lamb Steaks Alphonso

Eggplant is a very popular vegetable in Californian cooking. It goes perfectly with lamb marinated with garlic and rosemary.

PREPARATION TIME: 1 hour
COOKING TIME: 20 minutes

---

4 large or 8 small round bone lamb
   steaks
4 tbsps olive oil
1 clove garlic, crushed
1 sprig fresh rosemary
Black pepper
1 tbsp red wine vinegar
1 large eggplant
Salt
4 tbsps olive oil

1 small green pepper, seeded and
   cut into 1-inch pieces
1 small red pepper, seeded and cut
   into 1-inch pieces
2 shallots, chopped
2 tsps chopped fresh parsley
2 tsps chopped fresh marjoram
6 tbsps dry white wine
Salt and pepper

Place the lamb steaks in a shallow dish with the oil, garlic, rosemary, pepper and vinegar and turn frequently to marinate for 1 hour.

Cut the eggplant in half and score lightly. Sprinkle with salt and leave to stand on paper towels for about 30 minutes. Rinse well and pat dry. Cut the eggplant into 1-inch pieces. Heat the second 4 tbsps oil in a frying pan and add the eggplant. Cook, stirring frequently, over moderate heat until lightly browned. Add the peppers, shallots and herbs, and cook a further 5 minutes. Add the wine and bring to the boil. Cook quickly to reduce the wine. Set the mixture aside.

Meanwhile, place the lamb on a broiler pan, reserving the marinade. Cook under a preheated broiler for 10 minutes per side. Baste frequently with the marinade. Lamb may be served pink inside. Serve the lamb with the eggplant accompaniment.

The jagged penninsula of Pinnacle Cove at Point Lobos State Reserve, California.

SERVES 6-8

Venison Stew

A recipe very similar to the country stews of France, this one made use of the abundant game found in the New England colonies.

PREPARATION TIME: 30 minutes, plus overnight marinating
COOKING TIME: 2¼ hours

3lbs venison shoulder or leg, cut into 2-inch pieces
2 cups dry red wine
4 tbsps red wine vinegar
1 bay leaf
2 tsps chopped fresh thyme or 1 tsp dried thyme
6 juniper berries, crushed
3 whole allspice berries

6 black peppercorns
1 clove garlic, crushed
4 tbsps oil
2 carrots, cut into strips
1 onion, thinly sliced
2 sticks celery, cut into strips
2 cups mushrooms, sliced
Chopped parsley to garnish

Combine the wine, vinegar, bay leaf, thyme, juniper berries, allspice, peppercorns and garlic with the venison, and marinate overnight.

Remove the meat from the marinade and pat dry on paper towels. Reserve the marinade for later use. Heat the oil in a heavy frying pan or casserole and brown the venison on all sides over a very high heat. Brown in several small batches if necessary. Remove the venison and lower the heat. If using a frying pan, transfer the venison to an ovenproof casserole.

Lower the heat and brown the vegetables in the oil until golden. Sprinkle over the flour and cook until the flour browns lightly. Combine the vegetables with the venison and add the reserved marinade. Cover and cook the stew in a preheated 300°F oven for about 2 hours.

Fifteen minutes before the end of cooking time, add the mushrooms and continue cooking until the meat is tender. Garnish with parsley before serving.

Facing page: Flying the flag in Cape May, an elegant New Jersey resort whose architecture is predominantly Victorian.

SERVES 4

Braised Rabbit with Peppers

Rabbit was a staple in the diets of the early Cajun settlers, who used local ingredients to vary this classic French game stew.

PREPARATION TIME: 25 minutes, plus overnight soaking
COOKING TIME: 50-60 minutes

2¼lbs rabbit joints
1 lemon slice
Flour for dredging
Pinch salt and pepper
1 tsp dry mustard
1 tsp paprika
¼ tsp each cayenne, white and
    black pepper
1 tsp garlic powder
¼ tsp dried dill

Oil for frying
1 onion, thinly sliced
1 small green pepper, seeded and
    thinly sliced
1 small red pepper, seeded and
    thinly sliced
14oz canned tomatoes
1 cup chicken stock
4 tbsps dry white wine
1 bay leaf

Soak the rabbit overnight with the lemon slice in cold water to cover. Drain the rabbit and pat dry with paper towels. Combine the flour, spices, herbs and seasoning and dredge the rabbit joints in the mixture. Heat the oil and fry the rabbit on all sides until golden brown. Remove to a plate.

Cook the onion and peppers for about 1 minute. Add the tomatoes, stock and bay leaf and bring to the boil. Return the rabbit to the pan and spoon over the sauce. Partially cover and cook over a gentle heat until tender, about 45-50 minutes. Add the wine during the last 10 minutes of cooking. Remove the bay leaf before serving.

The waters of Lake Malone reflect a sadly dilapidated Kentucky barn.

SERVES 4-6

Chicken and Sausage Jambalaya

A jambalaya varies according to what the cook has to hand. It could contain seafood, ham, poultry, sausage or a tasty mixture of any of these.

PREPARATION TIME: 35-40 minutes
COOKING TIME: 20-25 minutes

3lbs chicken portions, skinned, boned, and cut into cubes
3 tbsps butter or margarine
1 large onion, roughly chopped
3 sticks celery, roughly chopped
1 large green pepper, seeded and roughly chopped
1 clove garlic, crushed
1 tsp each cayenne, white and black pepper

1 cup uncooked rice
14oz canned tomatoes
6oz smoked sausage, cut into ½-inch dice
3 cups chicken stock
Salt
Chopped parsley

Use the chicken bones, skins, onion and celery trimmings to make stock. Cover the ingredients with water, bring to the boil and then simmer slowly for 1 hour. Strain and reserve.

Melt the butter or margarine in a large saucepan and add the onion. Cook slowly to brown and then add the celery, green pepper and garlic and cook briefly. Add the three kinds of pepper and the rice, stirring to mix well. Add the chicken, tomatoes, sausage and stock and mix in well. Bring to the boil, then reduce the heat to simmering and cook about 20-25 minutes, stirring occasionally until the chicken is done and the rice is tender. The rice should have absorbed most of the liquid by the time it has cooked.

Facing page: Monticello, Thomas Jefferson's remarkable house in Virginia.

SERVES 4

Chicken with Red Peppers

Easy as this recipe is, it looks and tastes good enough for guests. The warm taste of roasted red peppers is typically Tex-Mex.

PREPARATION TIME: 35-40 minutes
COOKING TIME: 30 minutes, in total

---

4 large red peppers
4 skinned and boned chicken
    breasts
1½ tbsps oil
Salt and pepper

1 clove garlic, finely chopped
3 tbsps white wine vinegar
2 green onions, finely chopped
Sage leaves for garnish

Cut the peppers in half and remove the cores, pith and seeds. Flatten the peppers with the palm of your hand and brush the skin sides lightly with oil. Place the peppers skin side up on the rack of a preheated broiler and cook about 2 inches away from the heat source until the skins are well blistered and charred. Wrap the peppers in a clean towel and allow them to stand until cool. Peel off the skins with a small vegetable knife. Cut into thin strips and set aside.

Place the chicken breasts between two sheets of plastic wrap and flatten by hitting with a rolling pin or metal mallet. Heat the oil in a large frying pan. Season the chicken breasts on both sides and place in the hot oil. Cook 5 minutes, turn over and cook until tender and lightly browned. Remove the chicken and keep it warm. Add the pepper strips, garlic, vinegar and green onions to the pan and cook briefly until the vinegar loses its strong aroma.

Slice the chicken breasts across the grain into ¼-inch-thick slices and arrange on serving plates. Spoon over the pan juices. Arrange the pepper mixture over the chicken and garnish with the sage leaves.

SERVES 4

Chicken Fricassee

This white stew is French in origin, but is reminiscent of Shaker or Amish cooking in its simple treatment of wholesome ingredients.

PREPARATION TIME: 30 minutes
COOKING TIME: 30-40 minutes

¼ cup butter or margarine
3lb chicken, quartered and
   skinned
2 tbsps flour
2 cups chicken stock
1 bouquet garni
12-16 small onions, peeled
12oz button mushrooms, whole if
   small, quartered if large

Juice and grated rind of ½ lemon
2 egg yolks
⅓ cup heavy cream
2 tbsps chopped parsley and thyme
Salt and pepper
3 tbsps milk (optional)
Garnish with lemon slices

Melt 3 tbsps of the butter in a large sauté pan or frying pan. Place in the chicken in 1 layer and cook over gentle heat for about 5 minutes, or until the chicken is no longer pink. Do not allow the chicken to brown. If necessary, cook the chicken in two batches. When the chicken is sufficiently cooked, remove it from the pan and set aside.

Stir the flour into the butter remaining in the pan and cook over very low heat, stirring continuously for about 1 minute, or until it is a pale straw color. Remove the pan from the heat and gradually beat in the chicken stock. When blended smoothly, add the lemon juice and rind, return the pan to the heat and bring to the boil, beating constantly. Reduce the heat and allow the sauce to simmer for 1 minute.

Return the chicken to the pan with any juices that have accumulated and add the bouquet garni. The sauce should almost cover the chicken. If it does not, add more stock or water. Bring to the boil, cover the pan and reduce the heat. Allow the chicken to simmer gently for 30 minutes.

Meanwhile, melt the remaining butter in a small frying pan, add the onions, cover and cook very gently for 10 minutes. Do not allow the onions to brown. Remove the onions from the pan with a draining spoon and add to the chicken. Cook the mushrooms in the remaining butter for 2 minutes. Set the mushrooms aside and add them to the chicken 10 minutes before the end of cooking.

Test the chicken by piercing a thigh portion with a sharp knife. If the juices run clear, the chicken is cooked. Transfer chicken and vegetables to a serving plate and discard the bouquet garni. Skim the sauce of any fat and boil it rapidly to reduce by almost half.

Blend the egg yolks and cream together and beat in several spoonfuls of the hot sauce. Return the egg yolk and cream mixture to the remaining sauce and cook gently for 2-3 minutes. Stir the sauce constantly and do not allow it to boil. If very thick, add milk. Adjust the seasoning, stir in the parsley and spoon over the chicken in a serving dish. Garnish with lemon slices.

Top left: the Kiamichi River near Rattan, Oklahoma. Top right: Yellowstone National Park, Wyoming. Above: the impressive rock formations of Monument Valley.

The world-famous neon lights of Las Vegas.

SERVES 6

Chicken Jubilee

California cooks are creative trendsetters. Trust them to change a famous cherry dessert into a savory recipe for chicken.

PREPARATION TIME: 10 minutes
COOKING TIME: 20 minutes

---

6 chicken breasts, skinned and
  boned
Oil
1 sprig fresh rosemary
Grated rind and juice of half a
  lemon

1 cup dry red wine
Salt and pepper
1lb canned or fresh black cherries,
  pitted
2 tbsps cornstarch
6 tbsps brandy

Heat about 4 tbsps oil in a sauté pan over moderate heat. Place in the chicken breasts, skinned side down first. Cook until just lightly browned. Turn over and cook the second side about 2 minutes. Remove any oil remaining in the pan and add the rosemary, lemon rind, wine and salt and pepper. Bring to the boil and then lower the heat. Add the cherries, draining well if canned. Cook, covered, 15 minutes or until the chicken is tender. Remove the chicken and cherries and keep them warm. Discard the rosemary.

    Mix the cornstarch, lemon juice and some of the liquid from the cherries, if canned. Add several spoonfuls of the hot sauce to the cornstarch mixture. Return the mixture to the sauté pan and bring to the boil, stirring constantly, until thickened and cleared.

    Pour the brandy into a metal ladle or a small saucepan. Heat quickly and ignite with a match. Pour this over the chicken and cherries, shaking the pan gently until the flames subside. Serve immediately.

SERVES 4

Roast Quail

This dish is typical of the way in which the early colonists made use of the ingredients they found in their new home, in this case serving game with local berries.

PREPARATION TIME: 20-25 minutes
COOKING TIME: 20-25 minutes

---

8 dressed quail
8 thin slices pork fat or 8 strips
   bacon
Fresh sage leaves
½ cup butter

8 slices white bread, crusts
   removed
Whole cranberry sauce or
   blueberry preserves with the
   juice of ½ lemon

Remove any pin feathers from the birds and wash them under cold running water. Dry thoroughly inside and out. Salt lightly inside and place a fresh sage leaf inside each quail. Tie the pork fat or bacon strips around each bird. Melt the butter over a low heat and brush over each bird before placing them in a preheated 400°F oven for about 20-25 minutes. Baste the quail from time to time with the melted butter and the pan juices.

Put the remaining butter in a large frying pan and place over fairly high heat. When hot, add slices of bread which have been cut to fit the quail. Brown them on both sides in the butter and remove to paper towels to drain.

When the quail are cooked, remove the threads and take off the bacon or pork fat, if desired. The fat or bacon may be served with the quail. Place each quail on a piece of fried bread and serve with whole cranberry sauce or the blueberry preserves mixed with the lemon juice. Spoon some of the pan juices over each quail before serving.

Mount Vernon was George Washington's splendid colonial-style home in Virginiaz, and the house is now open to the public.

SERVES 6

Turkey Kebabs

Don't just keep healthful turkey for high days and holidays. Break with
tradition and try these kebabs.

PREPARATION TIME: 20 minutes, plus overnight marinating
COOKING TIME: 40 minutes

3lbs turkey meat
2 tsps chopped sage
1 sprig rosemary
Juice of 1 lemon
2 tbsps olive oil

Salt and pepper
4oz sliced bacon, rinds and bones
    removed
Whole sage leaves

Remove any bones from the turkey and cut the meat into even-sized pieces. Combine
the chopped sage, rosemary, lemon juice, oil, and salt and pepper in a large bowl and
add the turkey meat. Stir once or twice to coat evenly, cover and leave in the
refrigerator overnight.

Cut the bacon slices in half and wrap around some of the pieces of turkey. Leave
other pieces of turkey unwrapped. Thread the bacon-wrapped turkey, plain turkey and
whole sage leaves onto skewers, alternating the ingredients.

Cook in a preheated 400°F oven for about 40 minutes. Alternatively, cook for 30
minutes and place the kebabs under a preheated broiler for 10 minutes to crisp the
bacon. Baste frequently with the marinade while cooking. Pour any remaining
marinade and pan juices over the kebabs to serve.

*Facing page: the vast entrance to Joint Trail, leading to Chesler
Park, Utah.*

SERVES 2

Roast Pigeon with Juniper Sauce

The first settlers relied on locally caught game to survive, and this basically simple dish looks back to those days, while adding a touch of modern luxury.

PREPARATION TIME: 10 minutes
COOKING TIME: 40 minutes, in total

---

2 pigeons, dressed
4oz chicken liver pâté
1 tbsp brandy
6 strips bacon

SAUCE
2oz smoked bacon, chopped
1 onion, finely chopped
½ carrot, finely chopped

1 stick celery, finely chopped
1 tbsp juniper berries
2 tbsps flour
1 cup stock
½ cup white wine
1 tsp tomato paste (optional)
Salt and pepper

Pluck any pin feathers from the pigeons with tweezers or singe them over a gas flame.

Mix the pâté and brandy together and spread on the insides of each pigeon. Tie the bacon on the pigeons to cover the breasts and roast them in a preheated 400°F oven for 35-40 minutes.

Meanwhile, place the chopped bacon in a heavy-based saucepan over low heat. Cook slowly to render the fat. Add the vegetables and juniper berries and cook until the vegetables begin to brown lightly. Add the flour and cook until golden brown. Pour on the stock gradually, stirring continuously. Bring to a boil and reduce the heat to simmer. Partially cover the pan and cook slowly for about 20-25 minutes. Add more stock or water as necessary.

Skim the fat from the roasting pan and discard it. Add the pan juices to the sauce and pour in the juices from the cavity of each pigeon. Strain the sauce into a clean pan and add the wine and tomato paste, if using. Bring to a boil for about 3 minutes to reduce slightly. Season with salt and pepper and serve with the pigeons.

The aptly named Swift River flows through the Rocky Gorge Scenic Area in New Hampshire.

SERVES 4

Stuffed Acorn Squash with a Rum Glaze

Squash has a subtle flavor that blends well with other ingredients.

PREPARATION TIME: 30 minutes
COOKING TIME: 1 hour

---

2 even-sized acorn squash
⅓ cup butter or margarine
2 cooking apples, peeled, cored
   and cut into ½-inch pieces
½ cup pitted prunes, cut into large
   pieces
1 cup dried apricots, cut into large
   pieces

½ tsp ground allspice
6 tbsps rum
½ cup chopped walnuts
½ cup golden raisins
½ cup packed light brown sugar

Cut the squash in half lengthwise. Scoop out and discard the seeds. Place the squash skin side up in a baking dish with water to come halfway up the sides. Bake for about 30 minutes at 350°F.

Melt half the butter in a saucepan and add the apple, prunes and apricots. Add the allspice and rum and bring to the boil. Lower the heat and simmer gently for about 5-10 minutes. Add the nuts and golden raisins 3 minutes before the end of cooking time. Turn the squash over and fill the hollow with the fruit. Reserve the fruit cooking liquid.

Melt the remaining butter in a saucepan and stir in the brown sugar. Melt slowly until the sugar forms a syrup. Pour on the fruit cooking liquid, stirring constantly. Bring back to the boil and cook until syrupy. Add more water if necessary.

Spoon the glaze onto each squash, over the fruit and the cut edge. Bake for a further 30 minutes, or until the squash is tender.

Facing page: the earthy colors and solidity of Dillard Mill, Missouri, contrast sharply with the almost bare trees.

Serves 6-8

Boston Baked Beans

The first American "fast food", these beans were frozen and taken on long
journeys to reheat and eat en route.

PREPARATION TIME: 20 minutes, plus overnight soaking
COOKING TIME: 3½ hours

1lb dried navy beans
5 cups water
4oz salt pork or slab bacon
1 onion, peeled and left whole

1 tsp dry mustard
⅓-½ cup molasses
Salt and pepper

Soak the beans overnight in the water. Transfer to fresh water to cover. Bring to the
boil and allow to cook for about 10 minutes. Drain and reserve the liquid.

Place the beans, salt pork or bacon and the whole onion in a large, deep casserole or
bean pot. Mix the molasses, mustard, salt and pepper with 1 cup of the reserved bean
liquid. Stir into the beans and add enough bean liquid to cover. Expose only the pork
rind on the salt pork and cover the casserole.

Bake in a preheated 300°F oven for about 2 hours. Add the remaining liquid,
stirring well, and cook a further 1½ hours, or until the beans are tender. Uncover the
beans for the last 30 minutes.

To serve, remove and discard the onion. Take out the salt pork or bacon and remove
the rind. Slice or dice the meat and return to the beans. Check the seasoning and
serve.

*Facing page: the rugged coastline of Martha's Vineyard,
Massachusetts, whose cliffs are famous for their startling colors
and archaeological riches.*

SERVES 4

Avocado, Orange and Black Olive Salad

A colorful salad that makes use of favorite Californian ingredients and displays all the verve of "new wave" food.

PREPARATION TIME: about 30 minutes

2 oranges, peeled and segmented
2 avocados
20 black olives, pitted
Basil leaves
½ small red onion, thinly sliced

DRESSING
1 tbsp white wine or sherry vinegar
4 tbsps olive oil
½ tsp mustard
Pinch of salt and pepper

Make sure all the white pith is removed from each segment of orange. Cut the avocados in half and remove the stone. Peel them and cut into slices. Cut the olives in half and slice them thinly or chop them. Use kitchen scissors to shred the basil leaves finely.

Arrange the orange segments, avocado slices, sliced onion and olives on serving plates and sprinkle over the shredded basil leaves. Mix the dressing ingredients together well and pour over the salad to serve.

Bixby Creek bridge on Highway 1 arches above California's spectacular coastline.

SERVES 6-8

Refried Beans

This is a classic accompaniment to both Mexican and Tex-Mex main courses be they poultry or meat, vegetable or cheese.

PREPARATION TIME: 15 minutes plus overnight soaking
COOKING TIME: 2 hours 30 minutes (maximum)
[Beans must be cooked at least 2 hours before frying]

8oz dried pinto beans	Salt and pepper
Water to cover	Grated mild cheese
1 bay leaf	Shredded lettuce
6 tbsps oil	Tortillas

Soak the beans overnight. Change the water, add the bay leaf and bring to the boil. Cover and simmer about 2 hours, or until the beans are completely tender. Alternatively, bring the beans to the boil in cold water and then allow to boil rapidly for 10 minutes. Cover and leave to stand for one hour. Change the water and then continue with the recipe. Drain the beans and reserve a small amount of the cooking liquid. Discard the bay leaf.

Heat the oil in a heavy frying pan. Add the beans and, as they fry, mash them with the back of a spoon. Do not over-mash – about a third of the beans should stay whole. Season to taste. Smooth out the beans in the pan and cook until the bottom is set but not browned. Turn the beans over and cook the other side. Top with the cheese and cook the beans until the cheese melts. Serve with finely shredded lettuce and tortillas, either warm or cut in triangles and deep-fried until crisp.

*The vastness of Texas contains many contrasts. Top: Big Bend
National Park. Bottom left: cypress groves on Lake Caddo. Bottom
right: Monahans Sandhills State Park.*

SERVES 4

San Francisco Rice

This rice and pasta dish has been popular for a long time in San Francisco, where it was invented.

PREPARATION TIME: 25 minutes
COOKING TIME: approximately 20 minutes

4oz uncooked long grain rice
4oz uncooked spaghetti, broken
   into 2" pieces
3 tbsps oil
4 tbsps sesame seeds
2 tbsps chopped chives

Salt and pepper
1½ cups chicken, beef or vegetable
   stock
1 tbsp soy sauce
2 tbsps chopped parsley

Rinse the rice and pasta to remove starch, and leave to drain dry.

    Heat the oil in a large frying pan and add the dried rice and pasta. Cook over a moderate heat to brown the rice and pasta, stirring continuously. Add the sesame seeds and cook until the rice, pasta and seeds are golden brown. Add the chives, and salt and pepper, and pour over 1 cup stock. Stir in the soy sauce and bring to the boil. Cover and cook about 20 minutes, or until the rice and pasta are tender and the stock is absorbed. Add more of the reserved stock as necessary. Do not let the rice and pasta dry out during cooking.

    Fluff up the grains of rice with a fork and sprinkle with the parsley before serving.

Facing page: cornfields stretch as far as the eye can see near Weston, Missouri.

SERVES 4

Okra Casserole

This vegetable is frequently used in Southern cooking and stars here in a
simply-prepared side-dish that is delicious with lamb or chicken.

PREPARATION TIME: 10 minutes
COOKING TIME: 15 minutes

4 tbsps olive oil
1 small onion, sliced
8oz okra
6 ripe tomatoes, peeled and
  quartered

Juice of half a lemon
Salt and pepper
Chopped parsley

Heat the olive oil in a sauté pan and cook the onion until soft but not colored.
    Remove the stems from the okra, but leave on the tops and tails. Add the okra to
the pan and cook for 10 minutes. Add the remaining ingredients and cook to heat the
tomatoes through. Spoon into a serving dish and serve hot or cold.

Charleston's oldest church, St. Michael's Episcopal.

SERVES 4-6

Caesar Salad

Both Los Angeles and Tijuana take credit for this salad, said to have been concocted one evening from the only ingredients left in the kitchen.

PREPARATION TIME: 30 minutes
COOKING TIME: 3-5 minutes

---

6 anchovy fillets, soaked in 4 tbsps
   milk
1 clove garlic, left whole
1 cup olive oil
4 slices French bread, cut into
   ½-inch cubes

1 egg, cooked 1 minute
Juice of 1 small lemon
Salt and pepper
1 head Romaine lettuce
4 tbsps grated Parmesan cheese

Leave the anchovies to soak in the milk for 15 minutes. Rinse and pat dry on paper towels. Chop roughly.

Crush the garlic and leave in the oil for about 30 minutes. Heat all but 6 tbsps of the oil in a frying pan until hot. Fry the cubes of bread until golden brown, stirring constantly with a metal spoon for even browning. Drain on paper towels.

Break the cooked egg into a bowl and beat well with the lemon juice, salt and pepper. Toss the lettuce with the remaining garlic oil and anchovies. Add the egg mixture and toss to coat well. Place in a clean serving bowl and sprinkle over the croûtons and Parmesan cheese. Serve at room temperature.

Top left: fall colors enliven the Green Mountains in Vermont. Top right: the quiet beauty of St. Francis National Park, Arkansas. Above: redwoods in Redwood National Park, California.

Falls Creek, Mount Rainier National Park, Washington State.

SERVES 6

Green Rice

Fresh herbs are a must for this rice dish, but you can use whatever mixture
suits your taste or complements the main course.

PREPARATION TIME: 20 minutes
COOKING TIME: 20-25 minutes

2 tbsps oil
2 tbsps butter
¾ cup uncooked long-grain rice
2 cups boiling water
Pinch salt and pepper

3oz mixed chopped fresh herbs
    (parsley, thyme, marjoram,
    basil)
1 small bunch green onions, finely
    chopped

Heat the oil in a large, heavy-based saucepan and add the butter. When foaming, add
the rice and cook over moderate heat for about 2 minutes, stirring constantly. When
the rice begins to look opaque, add the water, salt and pepper and bring to the boil,
stirring occasionally. Cover the pan and reduce the heat. Simmer very gently, without
stirring, for about 20 minutes or until all the liquid has been absorbed and the rice is
tender.

Chop the herbs very finely and stir them into the rice along with the chopped green
onions. Cover the pan and leave to stand for about 5 minutes before serving.

SERVES 6

Strawberry Shortcake

Summer wouldn't be the same without strawberry shortcake. Add a
liqueur to the fruit for a slightly sophisticated touch.

PREPARATION TIME: 30-35 minutes
COOKING TIME: 15 minutes

---

2 cups all-purpose flour
1 tbsp baking powder
Pinch salt
3 tbsps sugar
6 tbsps cream cheese, softened
3 tbsps butter or margarine
1 egg, beaten
⅓-½ cup milk

Melted butter
1lb fresh or frozen strawberries
Powdered sugar
Juice of half an orange
4 tbsps Eau de Fraises or orange
  liqueur
1 cup whipped cream

Sift the flour, baking powder, salt and sugar into a large bowl. Using 2 knives, forks or a
pastry blender, cut in the cheese and butter or margarine. A food processor can also be
used. Blend in the egg and enough milk to make a firm dough.

Knead the dough lightly on a floured surface and then roll out to a thickness of ½
inch.

Cut the dough into an even number of 3-inch circles. Re-roll the trimmings and cut
as before. Brush half of the circles with the melted butter and place the other halves on

top, pressing down lightly. Bake on an ungreased cookie sheet for about 15 minutes in a preheated 425°F oven. Allow to cool slightly and then transfer to a wire rack.

Hull the strawberries and wash well. Purée half of them in a food processor with the orange juice and liqueur. Add powdered sugar to taste if desired. Cut the remaining strawberries in half and combine with the purée.

Separate the shortcakes in half and place the bottoms on serving plates. Spoon over the strawberries and sauce and pipe or spoon on the cream. Sprinkle the tops of the shortcake with powdered sugar and place on top of the cream. Serve slightly warm or at room temperature.

Storm clouds gather over farmlands near Shaw, Oregon.

MAKES: 1 8-inch pie

Apple and Nut Pie

The addition of nuts and cinnamon adds new texture and flavor to an old favorite.

PREPARATION TIME: 20 minutes
COOKING TIME: 40 minutes

DOUGH
1¼ cups flour
10 tbsps sugar
Salt
1 egg
9 tbsps butter, cut into pieces

FILLING
1lb dessert apples, peeled, cored and sliced
¼ cup ground hazelnuts
1 tsp ground cinnamon
Juice of 1 lemon
3 tbsps apricot brandy (optional)
½ cup apricot jam
½ cup chopped nuts

Sift the flour and sugar (reserving 2 tbsps of sugar for the filling) and a pinch of salt into a mixing bowl. Make a well in the center and add the egg. Mix in the butter pieces, and work the ingredients together to make a soft smooth dough. Rest the dough in the refrigerator for 30 minutes. Grease an 8-inch pie dish. Roll out the pastry, and use to line the dish.

Preheat the oven to 425°F.

Layer the apple and hazelnuts in the pie shell. Sprinkle with the cinnamon, reserved sugar, lemon juice and apricot brandy. Put the apricot jam in a saucepan and heat until melted. Pour over filling. Sprinkle with the chopped nuts. Bake until the pie is golden and the fruit is soft. Serve either warm or cold.

Facing page: 333 Wacker Drive is one of the finest of Chicago's many modern buildings.

SERVES 4-6

Orange Bread Pudding

Bread puddings came to America from England and they remain as popular as ever in both countries.

PREPARATION TIME: 30 minutes
COOKING TIME: 1½ hours

---

4 cups milk
8 slices white bread, crusts
   removed
4 tbsps butter or margarine
6 egg yolks
3 egg whites

1 tbsp orange flower water
¾ cup sugar
½ tsp freshly ground nutmeg
Pinch salt
½ cup orange marmalade

Heat the milk until just scalded. In a large bowl, break the bread roughly into cubes and add the butter. Stir in the hot milk until the butter is melted and the bread has broken up. Allow the mixture to cool to luke-warm.

Lightly grease a large soufflé dish or pudding basin.

Combine the egg yolks and whites with the orange flower water in a bowl, and beat until frothy. Stir in the sugar, nutmeg and salt. Stir the egg mixture into the bread and milk mixture until just combined, and pour into the prepared mold. Cover the mold with lightly greased aluminum foil and tie tightly. Place the dish on a rack in a large saucepan and fill with boiling water to within 1 inch of the top of the bowl. Bring the water to boiling and then allow to simmer, covered, for 1½ hours, or until the pudding is firm in the center.

Allow to cool for about 30 minutes and then loosen the edge with a knife. Invert onto a serving plate to unmold. Spread the top with orange marmalade and serve warm or cold.

Manhattan's spectacular skyline at sunset, when the city shimmers with the lights of buildings, cars and streets.

SERVES 6

Apple Filled Pancakes

German immigrants brought this recipe to New England, where it was
invaluable for using the fall apple crop.

PREPARATION TIME: 30 minutes
COOKING TIME: 10 minutes for the filling,
5-6 minutes per pancake

FILLING
3 tbsps butter or margarine
1½lbs cooking apples, peeled,
　cored and cut into ¼-inch-
　thick wedges
2 tbsps brown sugar
½ tsp ground allspice

PANCAKES
4 eggs
1½ cups milk
½ cup all-purpose flour
½ tbsp sugar
Pinch salt
6 tbsps butter or margarine
Powdered sugar

Melt the butter for the filling in a large frying pan over moderate heat. When just
foaming, add the apples and sprinkle with sugar and allspice. Cook, stirring
occasionally, until the apples are lightly browned and slightly softened. Put the apples
aside while preparing the batter.

　Combine the eggs and the milk in a large bowl and beat thoroughly. Sift the flour
with the sugar and salt and add to the eggs gradually, beating constantly. Alternatively,
combine all the ingredients in a food processor and work until just smooth.

　To cook the pancakes, melt 1 tbsp of butter over moderate heat in an 8-inch frying
pan. Pour in about ½ cup of the batter and swirl the pan from side to side so that the
batter covers the base. Scatter over some of the filling and cook the pancake for about
3 minutes. Pour another ½ cup of the batter over the apples and place under a
preheated broiler for about 1-2 minutes, or until the top is golden brown and firm to
the touch. Loosen the sides and the base of the pancake and slide it onto a heated
serving dish. Add 1 tbsp of butter to the pan for each pancake. Just before serving,
sprinkle the pancakes with the powdered sugar.

A tranquil Amish farm in rural Pennsylvania.

*Maine is traversed by many rivers, among which is the Penobscot
(above left). Above right: the fertile farmlands of Maryland.*

SERVES 4

Bananas Foster

This rich concoction originated in a famous New Orleans restaurant, and is now a favorite on any Creole menu.

PREPARATION TIME: 15 minutes
COOKING TIME: 10 minutes

---

4 ripe bananas, peeled
Juice of ½ lemon
½ cup butter
½ cup soft brown sugar, light or
    dark
Pinch ground cinnamon and
    nutmeg

4 tbsps orange juice
½ cup white or dark rum
Whipped cream
Chopped pecans

Cut the bananas in half lengthwise and sprinkle with lemon juice on all sides. Melt the butter in a large frying pan and add the sugar, cinnamon, nutmeg and orange juice. Stir over gentle heat until the sugar dissolves into a syrup. Add the banana halves and cook gently for about 3 minutes, basting the bananas often with syrup, but not turning them.

Once the bananas are heated through, warm the rum in a small saucepan or a ladle and ignite with a match. Pour the flaming rum over the bananas and shake the pan gently until the flames die down naturally. Place 2 banana halves on a serving plate and top with some of the whipped cream. Sprinkle with pecans and serve immediately.

Facing page: War Eagle Mill, Arkansas, is one building of a picturesque little community beside War Eagle Creek.

SERVES 8

Caramel Custard with Orange and Coriander

Spanish in origin, this easy-to-prepare dessert was quickly adopted by
American cooks and is here given a new twist with coriander and orange.

PREPARATION TIME: 30-40 minutes
COOKING TIME: 40 minutes

¾ cup sugar
6 tbsps water
3 small oranges
3 cups milk

1 tbsp coriander seeds, crushed
6 eggs
2 egg yolks
¾ cup sugar

To prepare the caramel, put the sugar and water in a heavy-based saucepan and bring
to the boil over gentle heat to dissolve the sugar. Once the sugar is dissolved, bring to
the boil over high heat and cook to a golden brown, watching the color carefully.
While the caramel is cooking, warm 8 custard cups. When the caramel is brown, pour
an equal amount into each cup and swirl quickly to coat the base and sides with
caramel. Leave the caramel to cool and harden in the cups.

Grate the oranges and combine the rind, milk and crushed coriander seeds in a
deep saucepan. Set the oranges aside for later use. Bring the milk almost to boiling
point and set it aside for the flavors to infuse. Beat the eggs, yolks and sugar together
until light and fluffy. Gradually strain on the milk, stirring well in between each
addition. Pour the custard mixture over the caramel in each cup. Place the cups in a
bain-marie and place in a preheated 325°F oven for about 40 minutes, or until a knife
inserted into the center of the custards comes out clean. Lower the oven temperature
slightly if the water begins to boil around the cups.

When the custards are cooked, remove the cups from the bain-marie and refrigerate
for at least 3 hours or overnight until the custard is completely cold and set. To serve,
loosen the custards from the sides of the cup with a small knife and turn them out onto
individual plates. Peel the white pith from around the oranges and segment them.
Place some of the orange segments around the custards and serve immediately.

*The lighthouse causeway provides the ideal opportunity for
evening strollers to enjoy a hazy sunset in Michigan City.*

Above left: Hawaii's tropical sky at sunset, when the range of colors is breathtaking.
Above right: a delightful old house in Dodge City, Kansas.

MAKES: 1 pie

Black Bottom Ice Cream Pie

Unbelievably simple, yet incredibly delicious and impressive, this pie is a perfect ending to a summer meal or to a spicy one anytime.

PREPARATION TIME: 25 minutes, plus several hours freezing time

8-10 Graham crackers, crushed
½ cup butter or margarine, melted
4oz shredded coconut

2oz semisweet chocolate, melted
3 cups coffee ice cream
Dark rum

Crush the crackers with a rolling pin or in a food processor. Mix with the melted butter or margarine. Press into an 8-inch loose-bottomed flan dish. Chill thoroughly in the refrigerator.

Meanwhile, combine 4 tbsps coconut with the melted chocolate. When cooled but not solidified, add about a quarter of the coffee ice cream, mixing well. Spread the mixture over the chilled crust and freeze until firm.

Soften the remaining ice cream with an electric mixer or food processor and spread over the chocolate-coconut layer. Re-freeze until firm.

Toast the remaining coconut in a moderate oven, stirring frequently until pale golden brown. Allow to cool completely. Remove the pie from the freezer and leave in the refrigerator 30 minutes before serving. Push up the base of the dish and place the pie on a serving plate. Sprinkle the top with toasted coconut. Cut into wedges and drizzle with rum before serving.

Facing page: many of the lovely old houses near Brenton Point, Rhode Island, have panoramic views across the ocean.

SERVES 4

Mango and Coconut with Lime Sabayon

The taste of mango with lime is sensational, especially when served with the deliciously creamy sauce in this stylish dessert.

PREPARATION TIME: 40 minutes
COOKING TIME: 10 minutes

---

2 large, ripe mangoes, peeled and
   sliced
1 fresh coconut
2 egg yolks

4 tbsps sugar
Juice and grated rind of 2 limes
½ cup heavy cream, whipped

Arrange thin slices of mango on individual serving plates.

Break the coconut in half and then into smaller sections. Grate the white pulp, taking care to avoid grating the brown skin. Use the coarse side of the grater to make shreds and scatter them over the mango slices.

Place the egg yolks and sugar in the top of a double boiler or a large bowl. Whip until very thick and lemon colored. Stir in the lime juice and place the mixture over simmering water. Whip constantly while the mixture gently cooks and becomes thick and creamy. Remove from the heat and place in another bowl of iced water to cool quickly. Whip the mixture while it cools. Fold in the whipped cream and spoon onto the fruit. Garnish with the grated lime rind.

Old Faithful Geyser in Yellowstone National Park, Wyoming.

MAKES: 1 10-inch pie

Blueberry Pie

Americans love pie for dessert. In New England, where blueberries
flourish, it's only natural to find them in a pie.

PREPARATION TIME: 30-40 minutes
COOKING TIME: 50-55 minutes

DOUGH
2 cups all-purpose flour
Pinch salt
½ cup butter, margarine or lard
Cold milk

FILLING
1lb blueberries
2 tbsps cornstarch
4 tbsps water
2 tbsps lemon juice
1 cup sugar
1 egg beaten with a pinch of salt

Sift the flour and a pinch of salt into a mixing bowl. Cut in the fat until the mixture
resembles fine bread crumbs. Stir in enough cold milk to make a firm ball of dough.
Cover and chill for 30 minutes.

Divide the dough in half and roll out one half to form the base. Use a floured rolling
pin to lower it into a 10-inch pie dish, and press it against the sides. Chill the pie shell
and the remaining half of the dough while preparing the filling.

Place the fruit in a bowl and mix the cornstarch with the water and lemon juice. Pour it over the fruit, add the sugar and mix together gently. Spoon the fruit filling into the chilled pie shell.

Roll out the remaining dough on a lightly-floured surface and cut it into strips.

Use the strips to make a lattice pattern on top of the filling and press the edges to stick them to the pie shell. Cut off any excess dough.

Using your fingers or a fork, crimp the edges to decorate.

Brush the crimped edge of the dough and the lattice strips lightly with the beaten egg and bake in a preheated 425°F oven for about 10 minutes. Reduce the heat to 350°F and bake for a further 40-45 minutes. Serve warm or cold.

Mystic Seaport in Connecticut is a carefully restored nineteenth-century waterfront community. The Charles W. Morgan *is the last surviving whaler of America's old fleet.*

MAKES: 12

Corn Muffins

A cross between cake and bread, these muffins are slightly sweet and crumbly. Originally an Indian recipe, they've become popular throughout the United States.

PREPARATION TIME: 20 minutes
COOKING TIME: 14 minutes

---

1 cup all-purpose flour
4 tbsps sugar
2 tsps baking powder
½ tsp salt

1 cup yellow cornmeal
1 egg, lightly beaten
4 tbsps oil
1⅓ cups milk

Preheat the oven to 450°F. Grease a 12-space muffin pan liberally with oil. Heat the pan for 5 minutes in the oven.

Sift the flour, sugar, baking powder and salt into a large bowl. Add the cornmeal and stir to blend, leaving a well in the center. Combine the egg, oil and milk and pour into the well. Beat with a wooden spoon, gradually incorporating the dry ingredients into the liquid. Do not overbeat the mixture. It can be slightly lumpy.

Spoon the batter into the pan and bake for about 14 minutes. Cool briefly in the pan and then remove to a wire rack to cool further. Serve warm.

Facing page: the Coast Guard Station at Marquette, on Lake Superior.

MAKES: 1 loaf

Spiced Cranberry Nut Bread

Sassamanesh was the colorful Indian name for this equally colorful berry.
Here, it brightens up a quickly prepared bread.

PREPARATION TIME: 25 minutes
COOKING TIME: 1 hour

---

2 cups all-purpose flour
1 tsp baking powder
1 cup sugar
1 tsp baking soda
Pinch salt
¼ tsp ground nutmeg
¼ tsp ground ginger

½ cup orange juice
2 tbsps butter or margarine, melted
4 tbsps water
1 egg
1 cup fresh cranberries, roughly chopped
1 cup hazelnuts, roughly chopped

Sift the dry ingredients and spices into a large mixing bowl. Make a well in the center of the dry ingredients and pour in the orange juice, melted butter or margarine, water and egg. Using a wooden spoon, beat the liquid mixture, gradually drawing in the flour from the outside edge. Add the cranberries and nuts and stir to mix completely.

Lightly grease a loaf pan about 9×5 inches. Press a strip of wax paper on the base and up the sides. Lightly grease the paper and flour the whole inside of the pan. Spoon or pour in the bread mixture and bake in a preheated 325°F oven for about 1 hour, or until a skewer inserted into the center of the loaf comes out clean. Remove from the pan, carefully peel off the paper and cool on a wire rack. Lightly dust with confectioners' sugar, if desired, and cut into slices to serve.

Clapboard buildings in the quaint old town of Grafton, Vermont.

Above left: with its tall silo and red barns, this farm at Waterbury is typical of those found in Vermont. Above right: Chigrin Falls, Ohio.

MAKES: 12

Oreilles de Cochon

These light, delicate pastries have a rather unusual name – Pig's Ears! It refers strictly to the shape the dough takes when deep-fried.

PREPARATION TIME: 30 minutes
COOKING TIME: 24 minutes

---

1 cup all-purpose flour
1 tsp baking powder
¼ tsp salt
4 tbsps cold water

Oil for frying
1½ cups cane syrup mixed with ¾
cup molasses
3oz finely chopped pecans

Sift the flour, baking powder and salt together in a large bowl. Make a well in the center and pour in the cold water. Using a wooden spoon, mix until a stiff dough forms, and then knead by hand until smooth. Divide the dough into 12 portions, each about the size of a walnut. Roll out each portion of dough on a floured surface until very thin. Heat the oil in a deep-fat-fryer to 350°F. Drop each piece of pastry into the hot fat using two forks. Twist the pastry just as it hits the oil. Cook one at a time until light brown.

In a large saucepan, boil the syrup until it forms a soft ball when dropped into cold water. Drain the pastries on paper towels after frying and dip carefully into the hot syrup. Sprinkle with pecans before the syrup sets and allow to cool before serving.

A typical New England landscape at its most picturesque in the fall.

MAKES: 1 8-inch cake

Devil's Food Cake

No need to wonder at this cake's name – it's the ultimate temptation!

PREPARATION TIME: 35 minutes
COOKING TIME: 1¾-2 hours

¾ cup butter or margarine
¾ cup soft brown sugar
2 eggs, beaten
½ cup corn syrup
½ cup ground almonds
1½ cups all-purpose flour
½ cup unsweetened cocoa
⅔ cup milk
¼ tsp baking soda

FROSTING
1 egg white
1½ cups confectioners' sugar
1 tbsp corn syrup
3 tbsps water
Pinch of salt
1 tsp lemon juice

TO DECORATE
Chocolate shavings

Preheat the oven to 300°F.
    Grease and line an 8-inch cake pan with wax paper. Cream the butter and sugar together until light and fluffy. Add the eggs gradually, beating well after each addition. Sift together all the dry ingredients. Add the corn syrup and the milk to the creamed mixture. Fold in the dry ingredients and beat well with a wooden spoon. Pour the mixture into the prepared cake pan. Bake until a skewer inserted in the center comes out clean. Turn out and cool on a wire rack. To make the frosting: place all the frosting ingredients into a basin over a saucepan of hot water; whip until the icing stands in peaks. Remove from the heat and continue whipping until the mixture has cooled. Spread over the cake using a palette knife. (The frosting must be used as soon as it is made.) Decorate with the chocolate shavings.

*Amnicon State Park, Wisconsin, under a covering of winter snow
resembling the cake frosting opposite.*

MAKES: 1 cake

Syrup Cake

Rather like gingerbread, but with the spicy taste of cinnamon, nutmeg and cloves instead, this cake can be served cold with coffee or tea or warm with cream.

PREPARATION TIME: 20 minutes
COOKING TIME: 45 minutes

1 cup vegetable shortening	1 tsp cinnamon
1 cup molasses	¼ tsp powdered nutmeg
3 eggs, beaten	Pinch powdered cloves
3 cups all-purpose flour	4 tbsps chopped pecans
1 tbsp baking powder	4 tbsps raisins
Pinch salt	

Cream the shortening until light and fluffy. Add the molasses and beat with an electric mixer. Add the eggs one at a time, beating well in between each addition. Sift the flour together with a pinch of salt and baking powder. Combine with the molasses mixture and add the spices. Stir in the nuts and raisins and pour the mixture into a lightly greased 9×13-inch baking pan.

Bake for about 45 minutes in a preheated 375°F oven. To test for doneness, insert a skewer into the center of the cake. If it comes out clean, the cake is done. Allow to cool and cut into squares to serve.

Top: Minnesota's numerous lakes provide a peaceful setting for both fishermen and outdoor enthusiasts. Above left: Boise, Idaho. Above right: farmlands, North Dakota.

SERVES 6-8

Southern Biscuits

Hot biscuits with butter and sometimes honey are almost a symbol of
Southern cooking, for breakfast, lunch, dinner or all three!

PREPARATION TIME: 20 minutes
COOKING TIME: 10-12 minutes

1¾ cups all-purpose flour
½ tsp salt
2 tsps baking powder
1 tsp sugar

½ tsp baking soda
5 tbsps margarine or 4 tbsps
  shortening
¾ cup buttermilk

Sift the flour, salt, baking powder, sugar and baking soda into a large bowl. Cut in the
fat until the mixture resembles coarse crumbs. Mix in enough buttermilk to form a soft
dough. It may not be necessary to use all the milk.

Turn the dough out onto a floured surface and knead lightly until smooth. Roll the
dough out on a floured surface to a thickness of ½-¾ inch. Cut into rounds with a 2½
-inch cookie cutter. Place the circles of dough on a lightly-greased baking sheet about
1 inch apart. Bake in a preheated 450°F oven for 10-12 minutes. Serve hot.

*Facing page: the Governor's Palace, Colonial Williamsburg,
Virginia.*

MAKES: 24

Pecan Tassies

Like miniature pecan pies, these small pastries are particularly popular at Christmas in the Southern states.

PREPARATION TIME: 25 minutes, plus 1 hours chilling
COOKING TIME: 20-25 minutes

DOUGH
½ cup butter or margarine
6 tbsps cream cheese
1 cup all-purpose flour

FILLING
¾ cup chopped pecans
1 egg
¾ cup packed light brown sugar
1 tbsp softened butter
1 tsp vanilla extract
Powdered sugar

Beat the butter or margarine and cheese together to soften. Stir in the flour, adding more if necessary, to make the dough easy to handle, although it will still be soft. If possible, roll the dough into 1 inch balls. Chill thoroughly on a plate.

Mix all the filling ingredients together thoroughly, omitting powdered sugar. Place a ball of chilled dough into a small tart pan and, with floured fingers, press over the base and up the sides of the pans. Repeat with all the balls of dough. Spoon in the filling and bake for 20-25 minutes at 350°F.

Allow to cool about 5 minutes and remove carefully from the pans. Cool completely on a wire rack before sprinkling with powdered sugar.

Facing page: Hanging Rock in North Carolina provides an impressive view of the forests around Danbury.

MAKES: 24

Calas

These small rice cakes are crisp outside, soft and light inside. They are delicious served hot with coffee or tea.

PREPARATION TIME: 40 minutes
COOKING TIME: 40-45 minutes

1½-2 cups long-grain rice
1 cup all-purpose flour
1 tsp baking powder
Pinch salt
½ cup sugar

2 eggs, separated
6 tbsps milk
Grated rind of 1 lemon
4 tbsps raisins
Powdered sugar

Cook the rice, rinse, drain and leave to cool completely.

Sift the flour, baking powder and salt into a mixing bowl and stir in the sugar. Beat the yolks with the milk and add gradually to the dry ingredients, stirring constantly, to make a thick batter. Stir in the rice. Beat the egg whites until stiff but not dry, and fold into the batter along with the lemon rind and raisins.

Lightly oil the base of a heavy frying pan and place over moderate heat. When the pan is hot, drop in about 1 tbsp of batter and if necessary, spread into a small circle with the back of the spoon. Cook until brown on one side and bubbles form on the top surface. Turn over and cook the other side. Cook 4-6 at a time. Repeat until all the batter is used, keeping the cakes warm. Sprinkle with powdered sugar and serve.

The life of the early settlers is recreated at the Living History Farm at Des Moines, Iowa.

MAKES: 1 loaf

Chocolate Cinnamon Monkey Bread

Pull this bread apart to serve in individual pieces rather than slicing it.
Savory versions substitute Parmesan and herbs for sugar and spice.

PREPARATION TIME: 2 hours
COOKING TIME: 45-50 minutes

DOUGH
1 tbsp sugar
1 envelope dry yeast
4 tbsps warm water
3-3¾ cups bread flour
6 tbsps sugar
Pinch salt
5 tbsps butter, softened
5 eggs

TOPPING
½ cup butter, melted
1 cup sugar
2 tsps cinnamon
2 tsps unsweetened cocoa
6 tbsps finely chopped pecans

Sprinkle the 1 tbsp sugar and the yeast on top of the warm water and leave it in a warm place until foaming.

Sift 3 cups of flour into a bowl and add the sugar and salt. Cut in the butter until completely blended. Add 2 eggs and the yeast mixture, mixing in well. Add the remaining eggs one at a time until the mixture forms a soft, spongy dough. Add the remaining flour as necessary. Knead for 10 minutes on a lightly floured surface until smooth and elastic.

Place the dough in a greased bowl and turn over to grease all the surfaces. Cover with plastic wrap and put in a warm place. Leave to stand for 1-1½ hours or until doubled in bulk.

Butter a ring mold liberally. Punch the dough down and knead it again for about 5 minutes. Shape into balls about 2 inches in diameter. Mix the topping ingredients together except for the melted butter. Roll the dough balls in the butter and then in the sugar mixture.

Place a layer of dough balls in the bottom of the mold and continue until all the dough and topping has been used. Cover and allow to rise again about 15 minutes. Bake in a preheated 350°F oven for about 45-50 minutes. Loosen from the pan and turn out while still warm.

Gould Mountain and the sheer face of the Garden Wall tower above McDonald Creek in Glacier National Park, Montana.

SERVES 4

Tequila Sunrise

What could be better to serve as an apéritif to a Tex-Mex meal than this colorful cocktail?

½ cup tequila
1½ cups orange juice
4 tbsps Cointreau or Grand
    Marnier

Ice
4 tbsps Grenadine syrup

Crush the ice and place in a blender with the tequila, orange juice and orange liqueur. Blend thoroughly.

Chill 4 tall glasses in the refrigerator and when cold, pour in the cocktail mixture.

Tilt each glass and carefully pour 1 tbsp Grenadine syrup down one side. The syrup will sink to the bottom, thus giving the drink its sunrise effect.

The State Capitol Building, Montgomery, is one of Alabama's finest pieces of architecture.

*Above left: one of the many excursion boats on the Wolf River,
Memphis. Above right: Rivergate Plaza in downtown Miami.*

MAKES: 1 drink

Mint Juleps

The official drink of the Kentucky Derby, it's mint and bourbon with a
splash of soda – delicious but potent.

PREPARATION TIME: 10 minutes

---

2 shots bourbon
3 sprigs of fresh mint

1 tsp sugar
Soda or carbonated mineral water

Place 1 sprig of mint into a bowl, glass or jug and crush thoroughly with the sugar. Add
⅓-¼ cup of soda or mineral water, mash again and add the bourbon.

Pour the mixture through a strainer into a tall glass filled with crushed ice. Stir until
the glass frosts, or leave in the refrigerator about 5 minutes. Decorate the glass with the
remaining sprigs of mint.

*Facing page: the Kentucky Derby ensures that horses hold as
important a position in that state today as they once did in the
Wild West.*

MAKES: 2 cups
Red Pepper Preserves

This sweet but hot and spicy condiment adds a bright spot of color and
Tex-Mex flavor to any main course or appetizer.

PREPARATION TIME: 20 minutes
COOKING TIME: 20-25 minutes

---

5 red peppers, seeded
3 red or green chilies, seeded
1½ cups sugar

¾ cup red wine vinegar
1 cup liquid pectin

Chop the peppers and chilies finely in a food processor.

Combine the sugar and vinegar in a deep, heavy-based pan and heat gently to dissolve the sugar. Add the peppers and bring the mixture to the boil. Simmer for about 15 or 20 minutes. Stir in the pectin and return the mixture to the boil over a high heat.

Pour into sterilized jars and seal. Keep for up to one year in a cool, dark place.

The spectacular colors and rock formations of the Grand Canyon.

MAKES: about 2 cups

Hot Fudge Sauce

The definitive sauce for ice cream desserts!

PREPARATION TIME: 10 minutes
COOKING TIME: 10 minutes

⅔ cup unsalted butter
½ cup unsweetened cocoa
2oz semisweet chocolate
6 tbsps sugar

½ cup evaporated milk
Pinch salt
A few drops vanilla extract

Melt the butter in a small, heavy-based saucepan. Remove from heat and add the cocoa powder. Beat until smooth. Stir in the chopped chocolate, sugar and evaporated milk; bring to the boil over a moderate heat, stirring continuously. Remove the sauce from the heat and stir in the salt and vanilla extract. This sauce will keep in the refrigerator for 2-3 days.

Top: Dream Lake, Rocky Mountain National Park, Colorado.
Above left: a peaceful farm near Frankfort, Michigan. Above right:
icy waters near Port Wing, Lake Superior.

SERVES 6-8

Cranberry Orange Sauce

This North American berry, with its crisp taste and bright hue, is perfect with ham, chicken, pork and, of course, Thanksgiving turkey.

PREPARATION TIME: 15 minutes
COOKING TIME: 10 minutes

---

3 cups whole cranberries, fresh or frozen

Juice and rind of 2 large oranges
1 cup sugar

Pick over the cranberries and remove any that are shrivelled or discolored. Use the coarse side of the grater to grate the oranges. Take care not to remove too much of the white pith. Alternatively, remove the rind with a zester. Cut the oranges in half and squeeze them for juice.

Combine the sugar and orange rind in a deep saucepan and strain in the orange juice to remove the seeds. Bring to the boil and simmer for about 3 minutes, stirring continuously to dissolve the sugar. When the sugar has dissolved, add the cranberries and cook until the skins pop, about 5 minutes. Remove from the heat and allow to cool slightly before serving. The sauce may also be served chilled.

Facing page: brightly colored farm buildings in Bennington, Vermont.

MAKES: 2½ cups

Horseradish Pecan Sauce

This creamy, piquant sauce has a variety of uses. The recipe makes a lot, but a sauce this good won't go to waste.

PREPARATION TIME: 15 minutes
CHILLING TIME: 2 hours

---

1 cup sour cream or natural yogurt
4 tbsps prepared horseradish
2 tbsps white wine vinegar
1 tbsp Creole-style mustard or
    other whole grain mustard

Pinch salt, white pepper and sugar
1 cup whipping cream
6 tbsps finely chopped pecans

Combine the sour cream or yogurt and horseradish in a small bowl. Add the vinegar, mustard, sugar, salt and pepper, and stir into the sour cream. Do not over-stir. Chill in the refrigerator for at least 2 hours.

    Whip the cream until soft peaks form. Mix the chopped pecans into the sour cream sauce and stir in a spoonful of cream to lighten the mixture. Fold in the remaining cream and serve chilled.

*Top: Table Mountain, South Carolina. Above left: the beautiful
countryside around the Blue Ridge Mountains, Virginia. Above
right: farmlands near Mammoth Cave, Kentucky.*

MAKES: 5 cups

Citronade

Nothing surpasses a cold glass of lemonade in the summer. This is the
essential beverage of picnics and barbecues.

PREPARATION TIME: 20 minutes

---

1 lemon
¾ cup sugar
4½ cups water

Maraschino cherries
Lemon slices

Wash the lemon well and cut into small pieces, discarding the seeds. Place in a blender
or food processor with the sugar and 1 cup water.

Blend until smooth, add the remaining water and mix in well.

Pour into ice-filled glasses or into a pitcher filled with ice and garnish with the
cherries and lemon slices.

*Facing page: the quiet waters of Echo Lake near North Conway,
New Hampshire.*

INDEX